56 Days of August

56 Days of August

Ina Roy-Faderman, Paul E. Nelson,
and J. I. Kleinberg, Editors

Cascadia Poetics LAB • Seattle • Washington

Copyright © 2021. Individual works belong to their respective authors. All rights reserved. Second print edition.

Cascadia Poetics LAB
9030 Seward Park Ave. S, #213
Seattle, WA 98118
CascadiaPoeticsLab.org
www.PoPo.Cards

Cover Art: Doris Lynch
Cover Design: David O. Seaver
Book Layout: Lynn Houston

ISBN: 978-1-0879-8272-4

Printed in the United States of America

Contents

Introduction   15
    Paul E. Nelson

Mailbox 2016   17
    Mary Beth Frezon

Portage Glacier   18
    Elizabeth Aamot

Don't look for anything in my words   19
    Carolyn Adams

Bedtime   20
    Michelle Ballou

Warning   21
    Gabriel Cleveland

Texas Appetites   22
    Christine Beck

The Pitcher   23
    Jean Blakeman

Underwater Bar   24
    Rosanne Braslow

My Beautiful Backyard   25
    L. Lisa Lawrence

Banshees   26
    Nancy Canyon

Guess Who's Coming To Dinner   27
    Carol A. Kesler

Flamingo   28
    Catherine Carroll

Love Poem #2   29
    Rita Rouvalis Chapman

Beekeeper's Daughter   30
    Abhaya Thomas

Starfish   31
    Jennifer Preston Chushcoff

Evening in Moab, Utah   32
    Christine Clarke

You Live Here   33
    Tim Mateer

Deadhead   34
    T. Clear

Safe Interview   35
    Gabriel Cleveland

Sometimes, Abundance   36
    Diana L. Conces

Memory   37
    Laura L. Snyder

Poem for Rona Murray   38
    Linda Crosfield

Notebook   39
    Tanya Korigan

Perfume bottle (aryballos) with lion-head mouth   40
    Caroline M. Davies

In the Key of Commerce   41
    Roberta P. Feins

Confidential   42
    Pate Conway

Postcard Photo: La Louisiane, Cajun Cuisine Since 1881 43
Rupert Fike

Particular Mathematics iii 44
Vanessa Gebbie

Road Sign 45
Matt Trease

Goat 46
Alley Greymond

Monet's Garden 47
S. E. Ingraham

Untitled 48
Christine Hartzell

For Danae 49
Diana M. Herrera

abuela 50
Denise Hill

Golden Light 51
Kristin Cleage

Open Road 52
Janka Hobbs

Your Life, Reborn 53
Terry Holzman

Untitled [Herrick quote] 54
S. E. Ingraham

Frog Flower 55
Eugenia Hepworth Petty

Winona Minnesota 56
Treg Isaacson

Letter from Frida #31, 1954   57
   Judy Jensen

Protocol   58
   Alan Kahn

Bending Words   59
   Martha Jackson Kaplan

Visitors   60
   Christine M. Kendall

Ahmad Dances   61
   Carol A. Keslar

Calling Love   62
   Paul E. Nelson

The Wound   63
   J.I. Kleinberg

Grey Poem Two   64
   Tanya Korigan

Lacking the Exact Words   65
   Bonnie Wolkenstein

Poetry for Strangers   66
   Maxine Lang

Blur   67
   Linda Malnack

On Our Anniversary   68
   Paul Marshall

Grand Canyon   69
   Carmen Kennedy

Sturgeon Moon on August 18   70
   Lindsey Martin-Bowen

Star Dust 71
    Michael Martone

You Live Here 72
    Tim Mateer

Untitled 73
    Libby Maxey

Which Side? 74
    Alison Aske

Middle Finger 75
    Janet McCann

For the Swimmer from Singapore 76
    Amy Miller

Postcard Crow 77
    T. Clear

Postlude 78
    Kate Miller

Fig Jam Genius 79
    Paul E. Nelson

In Love, Everywhere 80
    Dairine Pearson

The Island 81
    Polly A. Pattison

Bruised Peach 82
    Kelleyanne Pearce

Papered Walls 83
    Eugenia Hepworth Petty

Sandhills Hornet Nest 84
    Amy Miller

Stabs of Memory 85
C.J. Prince

Tolstoi Becomes a Pilgrim 86
Will Reger

The Muse 87
Bethany Reid

Yarn Aisle, JoAnn Fabrics, Mid-August 88
Katrina Roberts

For Your Eyes Only 89
Kelleyanne Pearce

What If 90
Laura Rodley

Yew 91
Ina Roy-Faderman

Drowning on a Sunday Morning 92
Somdutta Sarkar

Luddington Lighthouse 93
Doris Lynch

Dear Juan Letter 94
Laura L. Snyder

Golden Gate Bridge 95
Stephen Sossaman

Queen 96
Dave Stankowicz

Watermelon Smile 97
Charlie Stobert

Summer Reflections 98
Christine Clark

Conversation with koi 99
   L. Swartz

Blotter Art 100
   Abhaya Thomas

The Floods Come 101
   Joanna Thomsom

Fish Who Grow Into Girls 102
   Sharon Tracey

August 17 ☉ at ♌25°/A Circle of Neat Houses, Each One Identical 103
   Matt Trease

Addie 104
   Barbara Jean Walsh

Natural Geometry 105
   Bonnie Wolkenstein

Birds Are Entangled 106
   Gay Guard-Chamberlain

Swallow Spit 107
   Elizabeth Woods

Postcard for Paul 108
   Laura L. Snyder

For all the postcard poets, past, current, and future
— J. I. Kleinberg

Dedicated to the memory of postcard poet Bridget Nutting
— Paul E. Nelson

For Avrom and Nilakash
— Ina Roy-Faderman

To Liz
— David Seaver

Introduction

I'm not sure what the motivation was when I told Lana Ayers I wanted to do an August poetry project that involved postcards. She immediately said: "I'll help!" I know that I wanted to create something that would make poetry closer to the top of things to do during that month which, let's face it, should be a national holiday; all 31 days. The 3:15 experiment started by Danika Dinsmore was an August event for many years, and I participated for several years of that project, but waking up at 3:15am is not something you can do for a long time, hence the notion of postcards. Lana was able to translate my intentions into a very clear procedure. This was a real gift and sets up the underlying motivation for creating the fest, whether I was aware in 2007 or not. To write spontaneously is the most difficult way to write and yet when we practice this, like any act, it gets easier.

Quelling the editor's mind is a gift that will inform all of our writing, but it is deeper than that. Trusting our own impulses leads us to a more satisfying life, one that opens us up to synchronicity, to a deeper trust of process and to, as Keats called it, a "negative capability." The ability to stand in "uncertainties, mysteries, doubts without any irritable reaching after fact and reason." In short, being open. In the 1920's Heinrich Wölfflin talked about the open stance in painting as opposed to the closed. He said closed art was a "self-contained entity, pointing everywhere back to itself" while the open "points out beyond itself and purposely looks limitless…"

So a taste of infinity awaits you in these pages and hopefully a sense of that August pace, lazy days when we can sip Old Crow, notice the Sturgeon Moon or the chatter of cicadas, at least in the Northern Hemisphere. The poet's job is to sink as much of their being into the experience of August and to give you a taste. In this age of instant communication that still is not fast enough, we hope you read this book and never look at postcards the same way again. Or as one letter carrier was overhead saying: "Hey, this one is pretty good!"

Paul E. Nelson
Seattle, WA
7.30.17

Mailbox 2016
    Mary Beth Frezon

Portage Glacier
Elizabeth Aamot

Of course I can't help but wonder
if any of this ice is still frozen,
whether already it has receded,
flowed into the ocean, become another
mere drop, exposing bare rock. It's like
all the potential I remember stored up
inside me that winter I visited Alaska,
before the man I met there came
to click his shutter, freeze the image
of my young face before the certain,
inevitable grief, before my son's diagnosis,
before everything I imagined for my life
melted into nothing but salt water,
cold tears. Where is that man now?
Back on the tundra, making postcards
of a different tragedy? The landscape erodes,
always exposing another layer,
even deeper, even harder than ice.

Don't Look for Anything in My Words
Carolyn Adams

my eyes will tell you more.
I may say ~
chocolate,
late,
redemption,
but I'll be looking
like I'm in love.
You may hear ~
galliard,
drunken,
wish,
but the colors
in my eyes
will mimic the last sunset
that covered me in light.
Will you say, in response ~
candor,
chartreuse,
tenderness
when I ask you your name?

Bedtime
        Michelle Ballou

Now I lay me down to sleep
to shouts of explosion in the next
room. Boogie man lives under the bed.
Keep your hands under the covers or
he'll bite you if he can. Hide the Ouija
in the closet. The planchette is a heart
that moves to the answers yes, no,
goodbye. Reach for the fairy tales
under your pillow. The giant is
beheaded. Children turn into swans.
A prince rides his horse up a glass hill.
Pray that the sound of sirens means
help is on the way.

Warning
    Gabriel Cleveland

Texas Appetites
Christine Beck

Meet me at the Taco Trailer Park
in Austin, between the picnic tables
and the windows wafting jalapenos.

Meet me between empanadas and tamales,
our lips a-drip with deep fried meat,
chili peppers and salsa.

Meet me beneath the First Street Bridge,
clustered with 10,000 bats at dusk,
rousing for their nightly flight for food.

Meet me as we spread
our wings, voracious, united,
dying for a bite.

The Pitcher
Jean Blakeman

Hammel's posture is closed,
the left leg flung over towards third.
How will he throw to first
in time, having to heave
that leg all the way over, passing home plate,
the pitcher's mound, the grass
and its shadows? It weighs on him, the out
and its allure.

Underwater Bar
Roseanne Braslow

How could even Jules Verne
have envisioned such a place?
Would he imagine Rose
an underwater ballerina
with blue sapphires?
She dances in waves of light
as he orders another round.

My Beautiful Backyard
L. Lisa Lawrence

Banshees
      Nancy Lou Canyon

Scudder Pond's mud is pocked with raccoon prints;
masked outlaws holding boxing matches, a sound
not unlike mountain lions going in for the kill.
When I lived on the shipping lanes, the nightly
marauders stopped at my side door to open the compost
bucket. The cat pummeled the glass from inside, his yowl
both terrifying & disturbing. One eve I went after
the critter myself, slinging a flip flop in his direction,
thinking I'd scare him off. Instead the big guy carried
my shoe into the woods, munching his tasty dessert.
Summer's over now & coons in dens wait out winter.

Guess Who's Coming To Dinner
Carol A. Kesler

Flamingo
Catherine Carroll

The gullet goes
behind the trachea
& heart a bird's
has stones
to grind. In a true
representation
so would mine —
waiting like this,
always waiting —

Love Poem #2
    Rita Rouvalis Chapman

I won't be the one
To forgive you, honey-blooded
Man. You are north of
Me and the white
Season has begun. If
Your back glitters with
Lake water in the late
Afternoon sun, isn't that enough?

Beekeeper's Daughter
Abhaya Thomas

Starfish
     Jennifer Preston Chushcoff

Everything an
algorithm —
tide pools full of
pentagons, a five-point
symmetry.
Arms and petals,
leaves unfurl,
bound by a geometric
blueprint.
The architect has left
a mark,
signed every living
thing in phi and
Fibonacci.

Evening in Moab, Utah
Christine Clarke

This is where the night sky
splits open along its seam
and where the red rock
rises to meet it.
The wind ghosts the crevices
and the canyons echo with words
we have forgotten how to say.
Star dust, sing us back into red clay.

Green Thumb
Barbara Jean Walsh

Deadhead
    T. Clear

In the morning rush —
no time to snip
the wilted blossoms
from the viola.
They'll turn to seed
before day's out,
and my only excuse
for an end to blossoms
is that I sat down
to write this poem.

Safe Interview
Gabriel Cleveland

Humanize the violent man,
tousle his hair.
What drives his hands into fists?
Surely, there's someone in his heart
big enough to fight for,
someone made of sparks who lights
his gasoline veins, but does that
make his actions more benign?
Are those bloodstains or rose petals
in his wake, and if the house burns down,
will it matter that the match was lit
in a fit of passion, or will
the only thing that matters be the ashes?

Sometimes, Abundance
Diana L. Conces

We came home, car tired,
ready for sleep, chasing
sunset, and, turning at
last — how good it feels! —
into the driveway, stopped,
shocked, at the profusion
of purple blossoms on
the sage that yesterday
was deceptively green,
waiting, to surprise us
as we stepped, wondering,
onto the drive in our funeral clothes.

Memory
    Laura L. Snyder

Poem for Rona Murray
    Linda Crosfield

    post-card on the windowsill torn into two
    —"Ootischenie" Rona Murray, 1974

a gift, this tiny book of poems
you consult, sometimes, late at night,
for guidance or solace,
wonder if the flicker in your apple tree
descends from one of hers,
wish she could be here now,
see how the trees delineate the land
she sketched to life
with words I wrap around me,
snuggle in

Notebook
Tanya Korigan

Perfume Bottle (aryballos) with Lion-Head Mouth
Caroline M. Davies

She loved the perfume with its hints
of rose and jasmine
but it was the golden pot
with the lion's head
and nose like her dog
which won her heart.

In the Key of Commerce
        Roberta P. Feins

While she dreamed of being a musician,
she trained as a typist. Who would know
if her fingers moved to Schumann's rhythms
while she clacked "Dear Sirs, Your letter
Of the 17th inst. was received yesterday."?

Pate Conway
    Confidential

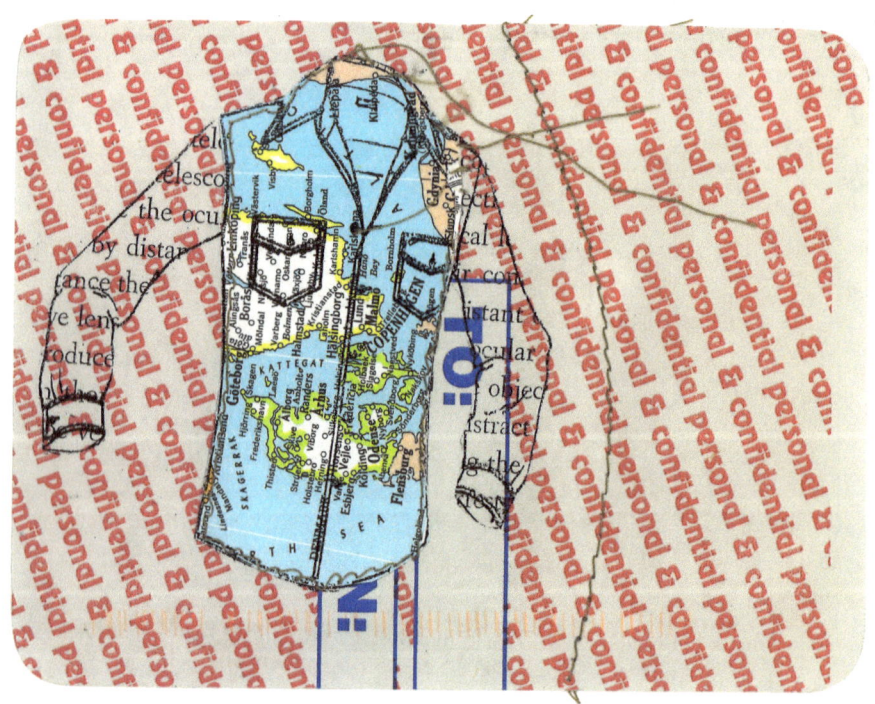

Postcard Photo: La Louisiane, Cajun Cuisine Since 1881
Rupert Fike

If I weren't allergic to shrimp
I'd want to be at that middle table
surrounded by etouffee-eating
bonnes aimees, all of us a bit buzzed,
but if one of them kissed me
I'd go anaphylactic on their asses,
and we'd all end up in the ER
at Mercy singing Hank Williams —
Son of a gun, we'll have big fun on the bayou.

Particular Mathematics iii
Vanessa Gebbie

The crowd, the tug from the centre
                                      to right
                    to left
always seeking   equilibrium,
never finding it.

The trio invariant principle,
                          two-valued
representation of   symmetries,

an entirely new type of particle
                            entirely new type

     of
  symmetry.

Useful for weak interactions. But

not love.   Never love.

Road Sign
    Matt Trease

Goat
Alley Greymond

I am a goat ruminating
on field grass and dandelions.
My teeth chomp, lips and bones
sliding sideways and you can't see
worry in my eyes.
Good thing for you my horns are hollow.
In any case, they arch backwards
as though confused about where I am going.
I am a goat and it is my black hair
floating in your tea, my hooves
not yours, tracking dust and dung
across the tapestry
you've been weaving for eons.
I'd give you milk and call it a day
but even that has soured.

Monet's Garden
    S. E. Ingraham

Untitled
Christine Hartzell

Hello,
I am having a wonderful time, except for
the rabbits. They ate the garden, then
they moved into my dreams.
Big round eyes
Peering through the shrubbery.
Soft whiskers brush my shoulder
As I write.

For Danae
      Diana M. Herrera

The rhythm follows you
As you stand up for your ancestors and
their children's children's children.

Bluebird at the kitchen table
As stories of Palomino wander
sacred checkerboard land.

My eyes have been closed to that sunrise.

abuela
Denise Hill

she watches telenovelas
in the afternoons
plays euchre at night
sipping Old Crow on ice
wakes at 4am 7 days
to walk dogs & feed them
for people who can afford
the luxury of owning pets
and paying for their care
she prays for them
at church on Sundays
may they all live
long happy lives

Golden Light
  Kristin Cleage

Open Road
Janka Hobbs

Drive enough miles
You will no longer be surprised
At what darts out of the trees.
Deer, vultures, people —
A puma bounds across the road.
There's a spaceship on a flatbed
Pulled off on an unmarked gravel drive,
And, just around the bend,
A grotto perfect for faeries
And a gingerbread house.
But most people drive on.

Your Life, Reborn
Terry Holzman

New eyes see new things,
Some beautiful,
Some sting.

Take off those
Rose-colored glasses,
Look at the masses
Of the multi-colored
Many.

See the dirty, deformed,
Diseased, and desperate,
Hold them closer to your
Heart than your
Lucky penny.

Then you will know the
Truest beauty.

It is not in the brushwork of
The master Leonardo,
Nor the majestic music of a
Mahler symphony,
                    But in the
Sun-fired palm of the
Old homeless man,
The one you see every day,
Reaching out to
You.

Untitled
    S.E. Ingraham

    I see a wild civility
    — Robert Herrick

Out the window of NYC's main library,
the one guarded by great stone lions,
with ceilings painted like cathedrals,
I saw Frank O'Hara strolling Fifth Avenue,
one December afternoon. He paused to buy a 'dog,
at one of the food-trucks near Herald Square and
was chatting with a homeless man sitting on a curb
there; they must've shared a joke or a funny story
I saw them both throw their heads back, laughing large
Then off went Frank walking briskly, whistling maybe—
I couldn't tell for sure. He stopped again and leaning
against a building I saw him scribbling in a small
notebook. Frank O'Hara—writing a lunch-hour poem—
I never thought I'd see such a thing.

Frog Flower
Eugenia Hepworth Petty

Winona Minnesota
Treg Isaacson

I lived one summer on a
boathouse on the Mississippi in
Winona Minnesota. My friend Dana
had introduced me to the owner
and he could tell I was heartbroken
and needed a change of scenery,
so he asked me if I wanted to live
with him there, floating on Latch
Island, the bell-like sound of flowing
water, white egrets gently springing
aloft or wading to pluck fingerlings
from the shallows, catfish attempting
flight, only to flop again into
their liquid world.

Letter from Frida #31, 1954
Judy Jensen

Gire la camara away,
friend. Estoy aquí
in the honeyed tarragon
on the tongue, tabaco loose
in a skirt's folds, tequila
en el suelo, the firefly's
darkness, sin parpadear.

Turn the camera away,
friend. I am here
in the honeyed tarragon
on the tongue, tabaco loose
in a skirt's folds, tequila
on the floor, the firefly's
darkness, unblinking.

Protocol
Alan Kahn

—After Michael Andrew's A Man Who Suddenly Fell Over, *1952*

When falling in public,
form dictates that one must avoid tumbling into
much smaller people
who may not recover from the sudden encounter
with a person of your intellectual heft, sartorial gifts,
and shining pate.
While some may rear back, fearing disaster, one must
always maintain an air of affable
bemusement, a gentle curve from shoulder to knee so as to
distribute the impact, and by all means, avoid breaking
the foundation.

Bending Words
Martha Jackson Kaplan

In Sumner, Mississippi
where Emmett Till's killers
went free, and deep-ditch bayous
stagnate along railroad track,
cotton-king, kudzu roads, I sat
in a heavily curtained parlor
in green-sticky heat listening
to my hostess, a social worker
in the Delta, rant on and on
indignant over an article
in the press about hunger
and starvation among children
in the Delta, black children,
of course. *No one,* she said,
dies of starvation in Mississippi;
they die of malnutrition.

Visitors
Christine M. Kendall

And so the guests have gone,
thank goodness for that &
the restoration of quiet mornings
without all that chatter &
someone turning on the television
to listen to news, or I should say
ad-libbing through it as if the inanity
of commentators is not enough.

Oh it is fine to have visitors come,
but finer too to see them go,
and to think my parents called me
the social one. They were wrong
about that, but how I would welcome
them back if I could turn back time,
watch their truck and trailer come up
the driveway, have tea with my mother,
offer my dad a cold beer and ask them
all the questions that now come to mind.

Ahmad Dances
Carol A. Keslar

—Ahmad Joudeh, Dutch TV Nieuwsuur, Aug. 17, 2016

Ahmad dances in the ruins
He teaches the orphans of Aleppo
and for a moment they forget
their families and homes are gone

Ahmad dances on the rooftop
Bombs and bullets in the distance
beat out the rhythm of war
"Better than a bomb," he says,
a stray bullet in his hand

Ahmad dances for his city
and the souls of the dead,
pirouettes through the ruins
of the jail where his uncles died
       and dancing, finds freedom

Calling Love
    Paul E. Nelson

The Wound
J. I. Kleinberg

We were wounded by fawns,
their tiny hooves pressed
in child flesh near our heart.
Was it Bambi, the Yearling,
who left that scar? or that one,

on my throat, that aches with tears
when the doe brings her twins
into the garden, crunches plums,
such modest recompense
for all her losses.

Grey Poem Two
Tanya Korigan

in anticipation of my tresses
turning the tide towards depigmentation
I want to expand the concept
of grey

let me embark on an age of
siamese-cat silver, quicksilver,
stormcloud back-lit by lightning silver,
grey of trout shine
ash from the fire that kindled your love grey

mellow mugwort, silver-mound Artemisia grey,
porcupine at a distance
pencil on paper grey

noon-shadow, storm sewer
church-spire,
mist, sea-smoke grey

pewter-bright, river by moonlight
all kinds of shimmery possibility in soapstone
grey

Lacking the Exact Words—Nenana River, Alaska
Bonnie Wolkenstein

Poetry for Strangers
Maxine Lang

The tourists say
They hate poetry—don't get it, they say—
Yet every summer they return,
Giddy to witness again the couplet of steady waves
The refrain of seagulls pretending hunger
The sunset's daily ode.

Blur
Linda Malnack

a black blur sudden and suddenly
me slamming on my brakes and the man
a leash dangling from his hand a black
leash and the car completely stopped
blur of a dog running and the relief
of the man with the leash in his hand
his hand with the leash in it raised
in a gesture of thanks mouth slanted
in apology and disbelief the dog still
running and the man running after it
and me moving again bags tumbled
to the floor spilled the dog the black
dog somewhere out of sight and
the man with the leash in his hand still
chasing the black dog loose and alive

On Our Anniversary
Paul Marshall

A planet spinning at 1800 miles per hour.
A photon of light traveling at 300,000 kilometers Per
      second.
You figure the chances
that a tiny beacon beam of light
will slip through a gap in our Venetian blind,
illuminating the arc of your hip
as if the Sun wanted me to notice what was
hiding among the loose folds of our bed sheets.

Grand Canyon
    Carmen Kennedy

Sturgeon Moon on August 18th
Lindsey Martin-Bowen

Such a moon to be named for a fish, red
as salmon leaping streams in the northwest,
where fish still thrive but not like before

conquistadors came and made the landscape
their whore by stealing gold, agate, lapis, turquoise,
and black gold spouting from earth layers eons old.

Tonight, a sturgeon moon shimmers over a black horizon.
Like a fish, it's oblivious to rubies, conquerors, and wars.
Even if it's the god Nanna, it can merely reflect light
       sent its way.

Star Dust
Michael Martone

I believe they might all
be gone now, these astronauts.
Returned to earth after
they returned to earth
in their star-spangled
contraptions, their sun
orange jumpsuits.
It finally all comes down
to scale and the light
years of distance we
travel as ash.

You Live Here
Tim Mateer

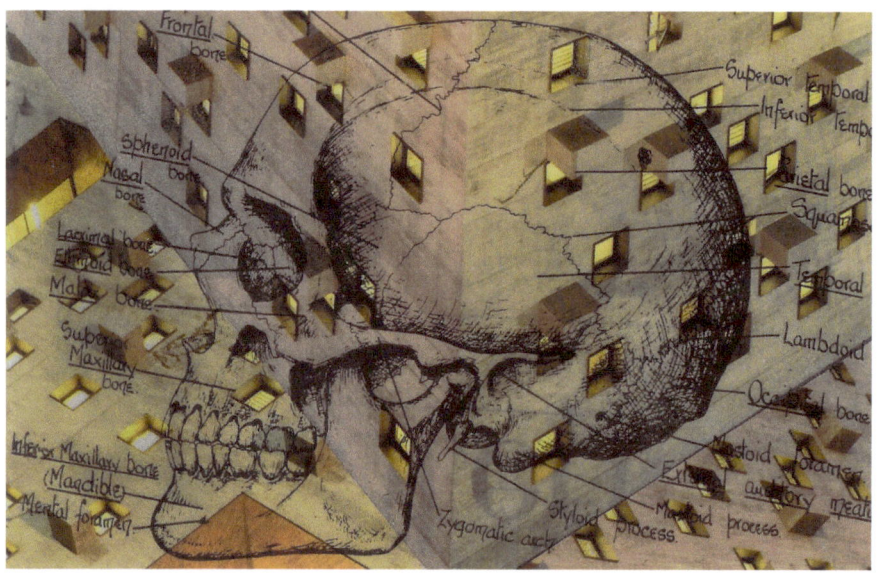

Untitled
    Libby Maxey

There's sumac where the house burned down,
against the still shut door
of one room standing.

No heat, no light, no welcome in its torches,
but the memory of flame.

Alison Aske
    Which Side?

Middle Finger
Janet McCann

—Postcard of Galileo's middle finger pointing upward, preserved in a case

HA! Gotcha! 500 years later
I give you my middle finger,
Although the rest of me is dust.
I lied to the Inquisition, took back
My heresy, and lived
Comfortably enough among my
Instruments, though under censure.
But I prevailed! The center of your cosmos
Was gone. And did you ever find another?
Did you?

For the Swimmer from Singapore
Amy Miller

—for Joseph Schooling

whose name the broadcaster only said
before the race because this was the finals
and everyone gets a mention, who did not
get the up-close bio segment so we don't know
if he swam nine hours a day for years
or almost threw up before the race,
who dove in that very same water,
whose body was a holy well-timed meteor,
who won and sang his national anthem,
which most of us had never heard,
after which the more famous swimmers
kissed their lesser medals for the cameras.

Postcard Crow
T. Clear

Postlude
Kate Miller

In Sitka ravens perch
on the steeple of the
local church, as common
as crows in the city.
My mother enters the sanctuary
and sits down at the organ,
the chords of her memories
float out open windows,
winging up like the birds.

Fig Jam Genius (for Jenn Miller, Kenosha, WI)
Paul E. Nelson

> *Who shall say I am not*
> *the happy genius of my household?*
> —William Carlos Williams

The happy genius of
this household cooks
w/ his black hat on,
cooks figs he procured
from the Fig Lady
(47th & Adams) to
make a grotesque
fig jam he'll eat
all week which will
smell like summer to him
& will be rejected by his
daughter who'll prefer a packaged
fig bar w/ sea salt & baking powder.

In Love, Everywhere
    Dairine Pearson

The Island
Polly A. Pattison

Years before,
eighty,
this was grass and rock
and then the sea
the house and tower exposed.
Now there are paths
cool dark groves
birds nest and call
their shadows soar and pass
all because someone
planted trees.

Bruised Peach
 Kelleyanne Pearce

So much depends
on a solitary,
bruised peach.

Left behind
on a country dirt road.

Pickers are come
and gone, heedlessly.

Papered Walls
Eugenia Hepworth Petty

I went within a caravan
of the old Egyptians
there was a hammock
uncommonly shaggy and thick,
and a crucifix of outlandish bone
fixed to a hook
on the papered walls
I took it down and held it
close to the light,
and the great flood-gates
of the wonder world swung open

Sandhills Hornet Nest
Amy Miller

Stabs of Memory
         C.J. Prince

I look at the date,
the tiny font on the lower
right of my laptop.
8.19.16
I wish to fast forward
out of summer's cloying
heat, to shorter days
where I write in darkness.
Skip the anniversary of the first surgery,
skip anticipatory grief, skip memory
of father's death, your death, forget
this weight in my chest.
I can skip nothing.
I listen to the silence of your footsteps.

Tolstoi Becomes a Pilgrim
Will Reger

This soulful Russian
put down his pen to take up
a pilgrim's staff,
to enter God where
he found him — the hills,
the village, the forest, or
on a muddy path.

I can finally see clearly,
he may have thought to himself
or said out loud,
on any given noisy night
in a tavern or in a marsh,

or standing at the open
refrigerator door, bare feet
to the cool linoleum,
a hundred years
in the future.

The Muse
Bethany Reid

On the last day, as on the first,
the poem is stubborn,
standing like a balky horse
inside the stable door, feet planted,
head down, and I have to sit
a long time, imagining myself
succulent as grass, my green tendrils
sweet with sap, before it ambles
toward me and lowers its nose
to my lips for a taste.

Yarn Aisle, JoAnn Fabrics, Mid-August
Katrina Roberts

Mennonite sisters
wrest
their eyes
again
from my
girl's
beautiful knees.

For Your Eyes Only
Kelleyanne Pearce

What If
Laura Rodley

What if you had been born
a horse, or just this January
in the blustery gales off the Atlantic,
what if you only longed for salt marsh
grass, the persistent roll
of the waves, its sound
as gratifying as rolling in the dust
on your back,
as much a part of your make-up
as your breathing,
the foal you are carrying
inside you, the words
you cannot speak
except to each other.

Yew
Ina Roy-Faderman

This is how I want to
get old: poisonous and
sweet, splitting useless
limbs as I go, succumbing
to nothing, breaking
from anything
except the earth, reaching up
only for the sky

Drowning on a Sunday Morning
Somdutta Sarkar

Sunday morning, I wake up restless from dreams
    of drowning off the coast of Mykonos
I wake up in the dark, gasping, believing I am there
    still, I cannot swim.
I wake up to the vibrations of the ocean floor, parched
    of throat, believing
that Triton and his forces are awakened, the guardians
    of the great seas stirring,
It is the morning alarm, hesitant and ensnared in the seaweed
    of the fading night.

It is Sunday morning, I throw open the blinds and the sunlight
    filters in
Softly, breaking the glass surface of the sea, or the sea surface
    of the glass.
The house is dark, cold, blue, like a giant fish tank,
    silent in its depth
I float through the motions of weekend living while the news
    anchor talks at length
of rising seas, melting ice, vanishing bears, that sort of thing.

Luddington Lighthouse
Doris Lynch

Dear Juan Letter
Laura L. Snyder

I choose Northwest trees;
Western hemlock, Doug Fir and
Western Red Cedar over
the juniper and dusty sage
of New Mexico. I choose
Mr. Rainier over
dried up gullies,
bare stones and mesas.
Cholla cactus cannot hold me
when mountain huckleberries
turn raspberry in Fall.
So keep strumming
your lonesome ballads
to sunsets orange.
Coyote will answer you.
I choose green moss
over rocks, and rain
enough for maidenhair ferns,
and flannel sheets for winter.

Golden Gate Bridge
Stephen Sossaman

If a poet whispered
"we are both
on the same side of the bridge"
what would she mean?

Some days I long
for the simple stone of
literalism.

Queen
Dave Stankowicz

Cicadas saturate
the sultry August heat
with noisy sex talk.

Watermelon Smile
Charlie Stobert

summer rain
brings
a plastic bin liner
worn as a rain coat
or
a boy with Down Syndrome
wanting to hold the umbrella;
a watermelon smile,
a murmur of
thunder

Summer Reflections
    Christine Clarke

Conversation with koi
      L. Swartz

You can't be a drummer like me.
You can't be a runner like me.
You can't buy a ticket or sing an aria.
You can't wear a tiara or ride a horse.
You can't type a paragraph or bake a souffle.
Band-aids never stick on your knee.
You're never going to taste good scotch.
An ofuro would make you say, huh?
A sauna would kill you.

Blotter Art
Abhaya Thomas

Suddenly the edges meant
as much as the center.

The scratch paper became
the art,
the blue heart of it all.

There was mystery in the mistakes.
Poem trash to be mailed.

The Floods Come
Joanna Thomson

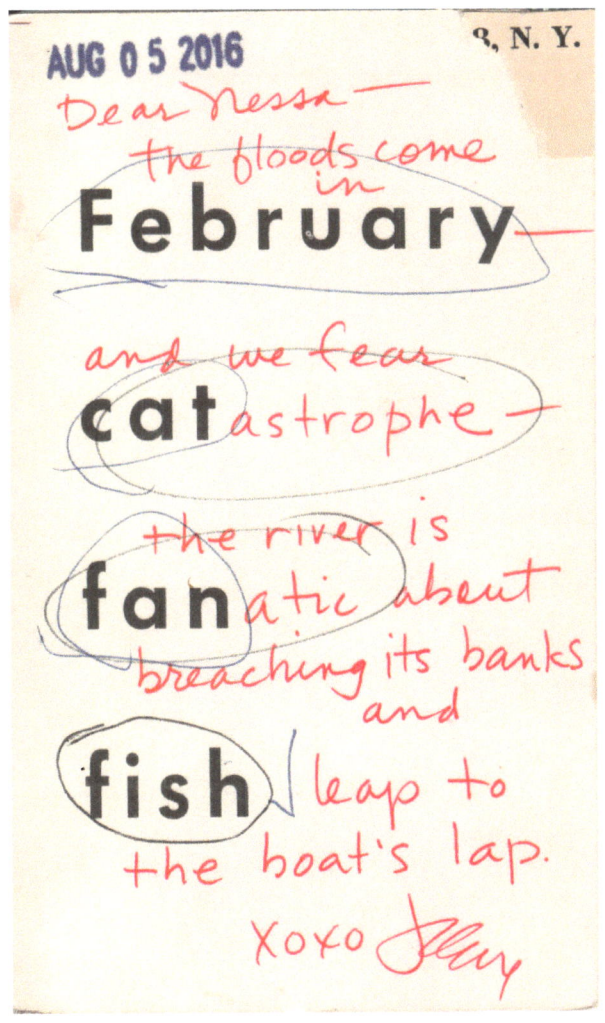

Fish Who Grow Into Girls
Sharon Tracey

Thanks for sending the baby picture—

my baby too was a fine fish
hanging pearly by her tail

with all that blood
rushing to her head

before she could clear her gills
and land upright, feet

planted firmly on the scales

her guppy mouth open
hungry
for the milk of air.

August 17 ☉ at ♌ 25°/A Circle of Neat Houses, Each One Identical
Matt Trease

Experiences do not add up
In these places humanity erects
the mind with no doubts making
the world
act like a clone of a prototype.
I am
a pyramid filled with scorpions
that ripple with permission to come out
spirited, imperious, demanding
a snake swallow its own
tail, a strange bargain
to deny the pain of Earth and to dream.

Addie
Barbara Jean Walsh

I carry Addie in my shape,
believing once if I reached her weight
that I could let her go,
but no.

She stayed,
rounding out my sharp edges,
filling my ankles on hot summer days,
giving me a glimpse of her life
through her gold pince nez
of privilege.

Natural Geometry
Bonnie Wolkenstein

The most angular thing in nature
other than those walking-stick bugs
must be the young boy
stick thin arms and legs
at geometric angles
wading out into ice-cold water
freshly flown over rocks
round and smooth from years of flow,
the kind of rounding out
the young boy's mother knows
sitting safely at the river's side.

Birds Are Entangled
Gay Guard-Chamberlain

Swallow Spit
Elizabeth Woods

'Madam, I promise you, it very good for you.'
He's trying to sell me the saliva of a swallow.

'Madam, it good for your lung, it good for your blood
circulation.'
These birds, swallows, make nests out of their own saliva.

'You see this nest, we already clean it for you,
then we make the drink.'
To drink bird spit? Swill it in my mouth?
Force myself to swallow? (No pun intended.)

'Oh no madam, the flavour it very good,
why you crinkle your nose?'
They say this saliva is a rarity, good for older people,
good for one's complexion.

'This good market price madam, Borneo price, please try.'

Postcard for Paul
        Laura L. Snyder

Contributing Poets

Elizabeth Aamot is a writer living in Oakland, California. Her postcard poems store transparent gravity, which she disperses as fuel to time travelers. To read mere transcriptions of the postpoems she has transmitted and to learn more about how you can join her timescaping efforts, please visit www.postpoet.xyz .

Carolyn Adams' poetry and art have appeared in both print- and web-based journals and anthologies. Recent credits are *Topology*, *Poetry Breakfast*, *Caveat Lector*, *Hawaii Pacific Review*, and *Remarkable Doorways*. Nominated for a Pushcart, she was also finalist for 2013 Houston Poet Laureate. She now lives and writes in Beaverton, OR.

Michelle Ballou's writing has appeared in *The Bellingham Weekly*, *Labyrinth*, and the Sue C. Boynton Walk Award. She enjoys close encounters with insects, moving authentically to dreams, and eating chili pepper sandwiches. She hopes to live long enough to experience extraterrestrial contact.

Christine Beck holds an MFA in creative writing from Southern Connecticut State University. She is the author of "Blinding Light," "I'm Dating Myself," and "Stirred, not Shaken." The former Poet Laureate of West Hartford, officer of The Connecticut Poetry Society, and poetry editor of the journal "Perch," she teaches at the University of Hartford.

Jean Blakeman lives and writes in Western Massachusetts, where she is inspired by nature, cities, and baseball. She is a fan of the World Champion Chicago Cubs.

Raised in the Catskill Mountains of New York, **Rosanne Braslow** draws inspiration from Hudson Valley lore. Her poems smack of the other-worldly and her horror stories remind us we are never quite safe. More short work by this author can be found on her blog: Work in the Margin https://writerose.wordpress.com.

Nancy Canyon, MFA, is published in *Raven Chronicles*, *Floating Bridge Review*, *Fourth Genre*, *Clover*, *Sue C. Boynton*, and more. For inspiration, Nancy walks to Scudder Pond daily, observing nature's seasonal changes. Inspired by her observations, she paints and writes in her Historic Fairhaven art studio. *Saltwater* is available through www.villagebooks.com.

Catherine Carroll Seattle resident, fan of birds, breviloquent. Poems previously featured in *Pageboy* magazine and University of Puget Sound's Dirt? Exhibition.

Rita Rouvalis Chapman's poems have recently appeared in *Bellingham Review* and *Red Earth Review*. She is a student in the MFA program at the University of Missouri-St. Louis and teaches high school English.

Jennifer Preston Chushcoff grew up in Southern California. After graduating from UC Berkeley, she continued north to the Pacific Northwest where she regularly frolics in the woods and water. She's an award-winning artist and author with work in anthologies, journals, and children's books. Science and nature spark her imagination. www.byjenn.com

Christine Clarke is a scientist and poet who lives in Seattle, Washington. Her poetry has appeared in *Clover*, *DMQ Review*, *Raven Chronicles*, *Poets Unite: The LitFuse @10 Anthology*, and others. She's been nominated twice for a Pushcart Prize, and likes to include aspects of the natural world into her writing.

A founder of Floating Bridge Press, **T. Clear's** poetry has appeared in many magazines, most recently in *Terrain.org*, *Scoundrel Time* and *Crab Creek Review*. She lives in Seattle and spends her days herding production assistants as Herder-In-Chief at a glass art studio.

Gabriel Cleveland struggles to be happy, but is usually quite content. He's almost always listening to music. He's come to accept that his life has value and wants you to know yours does too. He writes poems and makes collages in Austin, TX, where he supervises adolescents with developmental impairments.

Diana L. Conces writes poetry and fiction from her home in Round Rock, Texas. Her work has appeared in numerous anthologies and journals, in a major newspaper, and on a city bus. She has won numerous prizes for her poetry. Her photographs have appeared in *Peacock Journal*. Visit her blog at https://dianalconces.blogspot.com/.

Linda Crosfield's poetry has appeared in various literary magazines including *Room*, *The Minnesota Review*, and *The Antigonish Review*, as well as in several chapbooks and anthologies. She runs her micro press, Nose in Book Publishing, from her home in Ootischenia, BC, at the confluence of the Columbia and Kootenay Rivers.

Caroline M. Davies: Poet, poetry enthusiast and author of *Convoy* and *Voices from Stone and Bronze*. She blogs at http://advancingpoetry.blogspot.co.uk/.

Roberta P. Feins received her MFA in poetry, studying with Judith Hall, D. A. Powell, Carol Frost, and Alicia Ostriker. Her poems have been published in *Antioch Review*, *The Cortland Review* and *The Gettysburg Review*, among others. She has published 2 chapbooks: *Something Like a River*, (Moon Path Press), and *Herald* (Autumn House Press).

Rupert Fike was named Finalist as Georgia Author of the Year 2011 with the publication of his collection, *Lotus Buffet*. He has been nominated for a Pushcart Prize in fiction and poetry, with work appearing in *Rosebud*, *The Georgetown Review*, *The Southern Review of Poetry*, *Alligator Juniper* and others.

Vanessa Gebbie is author of one novel, two poetry collections and four collections of short and short-short fictions. She is contributing editor of *Short Circuit, Guide to the Art of the Short Story*, and she teaches widely. www.vanessagebbie.com.

Alley Greymond's poems have been seen in *Five Willows Literary Review*, *Rain City Review*, *Trestle Creek Review*, as well as other journals. She served with Red Sky Poetry Theater, The Washington Poet's Association, as Poetry Editor for *Urban Spelunker* and Associate Editor on *Open Sound*.

Daughter of a father who loved reading, writing, and reciting poems, **Christine Hartzell** has read, written, and recited poetry for her own amusement since she was a small child.

Diana Herrera is a member of the Klamath Tribes of Oregon, has lived in Washington State since 1977 and works in a non-profit that provides legal services to Pacific Northwestern Native American tribes. Having read and written poetry since childhood, she continues her education in creative writing through workshops and English classes.

Denise Hill is Editor in Chief of NewPages.com, an online resource for readers and writers, and a Professor of English at Delta College in Michigan where she teaches developmental writing, college composition, and world mythology.

Janka Hobbs lives in the Puget Sound lowlands, where she studies Aikido and Botany when she's not playing with words. Recent poems appear in *Douglasia* and *Grievous Angel*, and she has a story in the *Altenative Truths* anthology from B Cubed Press. Visit her blog at http://janka-hobbs.com.

Terry Holzman received her MFA (American Film Institute in Los Angeles). She is an award-winning screenwriter as well as a playwright, documentary producer, artist, and poet. Terry is a longstanding participant in PoPoFest, having written 547 poems (the last 120 on her handmade collage postcards) with an upcoming chapbook. She lives in LA with her husband.

S. E. Ingraham writes poems that appear in print and on-line, from Edmonton, Alberta. She's happiest when they reflect her philosophy: non-violent conflict resolution and peace advocacy. Recent successes? In *Poets 4 Paris*, her first poem published in both English and French; another, in The Persimmon Tree's International collection. More here: http://soundofthewordnight.blogspot.ca/.

Treg Isaacson is the father of three amazing children, grandfather to two lovely granddaughters, and grateful to live with his wife, north of Seattle. His work has been published previously in *The Monarch Review*, *KY Story*,

Motherlode, and *About Place Journal*. He anxiously awaits August and its postcards.

Judy Jensen is a longtime participant in the August Poetry Postcard Festival. Her poems have appeared in various journals and anthologies. She is a co-founder of the KinCity reading series, a letterpress printer with Float Press, and a regular volunteer at Poetry at Round Top.

Alan Kahn teaches High School English Language Arts at Garfield HS in Seattle, Washington, where he lives with his wife and 1.5 kids (College Boy rarely visits home these days, yet half his imprint remains). This first poem published outside of a workshop anthology thinks it just summited Everest.

Martha Jackson Kaplan is a Pushcart nominated poet who draws her palette from a passion for history, color, and a sense of place. She's a native of Seattle who has lived in Houston and Chicago, and now lives in Madison, Wisconsin. If you are curious for more, see: www.marthakaplanpoet.com.

Christine M. Kendall: I have done August Postcard Poetry for nine years and thank Carla Shafer for announcing this practice. It gives me incentive, and I love receiving poems. August PoPo has generated poems I've had published and poems I tinker with. I'm honored to have a poem in this publication.

Fascinated since childhood by the power of words and pictures to convey meaning and arouse emotion, **Carol A. Keslar** writes, photographs, and collages, to tell stories of identity and life passages. A former marketing and communication executive, she currently lives in Oakland, California.

J. I. Kleinberg See Editor biography.

Tanya Korigan works primarily in long form, multi-voiced, often interdisciplinary poems. The immediacy of the August form is inspirational, instructive, and a breath of fresh air. Each year it's astonishing that it continues to astonish but still, it does.

Maxine Lang is a poet, mixed media artist, and facilitator of Creative Journey workshops. She has enjoyed participation in the August Poetry Postcard project since its inception, and credits poetry for saving her sanity. A true beach lover, Maxine is grateful to be living and creating on Florida's Gulf Coast.

Linda Malnack lives and works in Seattle, Washington. She has published poems in many journals, including *The Amherst Review*, *Blackbird*, *the Seattle Review*, and *Southern Humanities Review*, as well as *Bone Beads* (Paper Boat Press) and *21 Boxes* (Dancing Girl Press). Linda is Co-editor of the e-zine, *Switched-on Gutenberg*, and Assistant Poetry Editor at *Crab Creek Review*.

Paul Marshall is a retired Community College Teacher living on Whidbey Island, Washington State. Most days you will find him playing ukulele, working in his woodshop, or writing. His poetry is published in *Blue Collar Review* and he has a book, *Building a Boat: Lessons of a 30-year Project*.

Lindsey Martin-Bowen teaches at MCC-Longview.
—*CROSSING KANSAS with Jim Morrison*: semi-finalist, QuillsEdge Books' 2015-16 contest.
—Work from *Inside Virgil's Garage* (Chatter House): Pushcart nomination
—*Standing on the Edge of the World* (Woodley): Top 10 Poetry Book 2008 (McClatchy).
—*Where Water Meets the Rock* (39 West Press)
—Publication in *New Letters*, *I-70 Review*, *Thorny Locust*, and others.

Michael Martone's favorite postcards were produced by C.T ART-COLORTONE. He lives in Tuscaloosa, Alabama with the poet Theresa Pappas.

Libby Maxey is a senior editor with the online journal *Literary Mama*. She reviews poetry for *The Mom Egg Review* and *Solstice*, and her own poems have appeared in *Mezzo Cammin*, *Crannóg*, *Think*, and elsewhere. Her nonliterary activities include singing classical repertoire and mothering two sons.

Janet McCann taught for 46 years at Texas A&M, and her most recent book is *The Crone at the Casino* (Lamar UP, 2014.)

Amy Miller's writing has appeared in *Crab Orchard Review, Gulf Coast, Nimrod, Rattle, Willow Springs, ZYZZYVA, Asimov's Science Fiction, Fine Gardening,* and *The Poet's Market.* Her poetry collection *The Trouble with New England Girls* won the Louis Award from Concrete Wolf Press and will be published in 2018.

Kate Miller lives in Bellingham, WA. with her wife of 33 years and her dog. Kate is a writer and a teacher who loves the sounds and meanings of words, both spoken and written. Her most recent publication is a poem in *The Raven Chronicles* journal.

Paul E. Nelson See Editor biography.

Polly A. Pattison is a teacher/naturalist for a small non-profit land trust. She has taught literature and music and art. She lives in the woods with her husband, indoor and outdoor animals, birds and plants. She has been writing poetry all of her life.

Kelleyanne Pearce is a postcard poet in the Pacific Northwest, which gives her inspiration and peace and is the place her soul is meant to be. She enjoys collaging, writing, and hiking. Her goal is to emulate Steinbeck's *Travels with Charley* with a teardrop camper, dog and cat in tow.

Eugenia Hepworth Petty is a writer, photographer, and mixed media artist based in the Pacific Northwest. Galleries and a list of publication credits may be found at: www.eugeniahepworth.com

C.J. Prince picks her own pockets for words, wears a shawl of metaphors and a wide-brimmed hat of grammar. Prince is author of the poetry book, *Mother, May I?*; a novel *Canvas Angels*; and *Twenty Four Houses*, a chapbook. Prince received the Distinguished Poet Award from Writers International Canada.

Will Reger was raised in the St. Louis, Missouri area. He teaches college-level history, plays many flutes, and is a member of the CU Poetry Group (cupoetry.com). He has been published most recently with *Front Porch Review, Chiron Review,* and the *Paterson Literary Review.* He can be found at https://twitter.com/wmreger.

Bethany Reid's most recent book of poems is *SPARROW*, which won the 2012 Gell Poetry Prize. She blogs at bethanyareid.com (formerly A Writer's Alchemy) and lives in Edmonds, Washington with her husband and daughters.

Katrina Roberts has published four books of poems and edited an anthology. She curates the Visiting Writers Reading Series at Whitman College, and co-runs the Walla Walla Distilling Company. Find her here: www.katrinaroberts.net.

Laura Rodley
—Pushcart Prize winner; quintuple nominee, Best of Net.
—Finishing Line Press nomination of *Your Left Front Wheel Is Coming Loose*, PEN L.L.Winship Award and Mass Book Award; *Rappelling Blue Light* also nominated for MBA
—Teaches memoir; edited *As You Write It, A Franklin County Anthology I-VI*, MBA nominee.
— *Counter Point* (Prolific Press)
—*Turn Left at Normal* (Big Table Publishing) forthcoming.

Ina Roy-Faderman See Editor biography.

Somdutta Sarkar is a communication manager by profession and a hodophile by passion. She writes poems for postcards, and micro-fiction and musings for *Terribly Tiny Tales*. She lives in New Delhi and is a citizen of the world.

Laura L. Snyder uses a slanted profile to scratch out words in hardback journals under Northwest trees. Find her latest writing in *Claudius Speaks, Quill and Parchment, Windfall, Labletter*. Recently, she had a blissful month long residency at Hypatia-in-the-Woods. Laura has two chapbooks of poetry, *Winged*, and *Witness*.

Stephen Sossaman, in Burbank, California, is the author of *Writing Your First Play* (Pearson) and the long-poem *And Job Lies in the Feedlot Where He Fell* (Inkonoclast). His poetry and stories have appeared in several dozen literary publications. He is shopping a comic novel set during the Vietnam War.

David Stankowicz is a retired educator. Currently he is writing American Sentences, poetry coupled with his photographs, a collection of Benny poems inspired by John Berryman's "Dream Songs," and his first novel. He lives on an island in Maine with his wife Debbie and two dogs, Grady and Jade.

Charlie Stobert was born in Australia, grew up in New Zealand and has lived in U.K. since 2001. He is an avid student of poetry, writing since university, and a regular participant in the August Poetry Postcard Fest and other literary events. He lives with his wife, Heather.

L. Swartz
—TL/DR: I make poetry + story + image + performance + found audio.
—Policies: Constraint is freedom. Art is for giving away and letting it find its proper home.
—Work: *Land of Lists* (Floating Bridge Press), *Deck of Shufflepoems* (Minor Arcana Press)
—Where I literally stand each day of the Trump regime: propagandaministry.tumblr.com.

Abhaya Thomas lives in unincorporated NW Portland Oregon on a small farm. Here, along with her husband, she raised four children, an occasional dairy goat and hopefully her consciousness. There have been a few artistic endeavors thrown in the mix. This is her first published work.

Sharon Tracey is the author of *What I Remember Most is Everything*, her first full-length collection of poetry (ALL CAPS PUBLISHING, 2017). Her poems have appeared in *Naugatuck River Review, Silkworm, The Skinny Poetry Journal, Haiku Journal*, and elsewhere. She lives in Amherst, Massachusetts.

Matt Trease is an artist and IT Analyst living in Seattle, WA. His poems have appeared recently in *Nautilus Review, Apricity, Hotel Amerika*, and *Phoebe*. He is the author of the chapbook *Later Heaven: Production Cycles*, and he co-runs the Margin Shift reading series in Seattle's Belltown neighborhood.

Barbara Jean Walsh is a writer, editor, and designer living in Springfield, Massachusetts. She is an active member of the Pioneer Valley Riverfront Club as a rower and manager of our Dragon Boat team. Since moving to Western Mass in 2015, she has enjoyed becoming part of the area's community of writers and makers.

Bonnie Wolkenstein is a writer, photographer and psychologist. Publications include *Drash: Northwest Mosaic*. Local readings include a featured reader at Easy Speak Seattle and the Rainier Valley Lit Crawl. Her poetry, essays and photography explore what lies below the surface of everyday moments and make their home at www.thinkinggirlthoughts.com.

Elizabeth Woods is a writer and poet from Sydney, Australia. Elizabeth likes dreaming, hiking, travelling the world, cloud watching, writing, building new businesses, long walks with Dodger her Cocker Spaniel, making mosaics, taking photographs, meeting new people and tapping into her creative soul. Elizabeth dislikes cold weather - brrrr!

Contributing Artists

Alison Birkmeyer Aske is a performer, writer, collage artist, and director. When she isn't writing or glueing pieces of paper together, she is teaching pilates or goofing off on the internet.

Christine Clarke is a poet and accidental artist who loves to combine forms in ekphrastic poetry and mixed media collage. This is her first published art piece. She'd like to thank Stacie Kentop for her encouragement and for providing access to the Art Room, where creativity blooms.

Kristin Cleage Born the oldest daughter of Albert and Doris (Graham) Cleage in Springfield, Massachusetts seventy years ago. Grew up in Detroit. Raised six children, goats, chickens, and gardens. All the while writing, printing, taking photographs, celebrating numerous family events and figuring out the puzzle of my family history.

A founder of Floating Bridge Press, **T. Clear's** poetry has appeared in many magazines, most recently in *Terrain.org, Scoundrel Time and Crab Creek Review*. She lives in Seattle and spends her days herding production assistants as Herder-In-Chief at a glass art studio.

Gabriel Cleveland struggles to be happy, but is usually quite content. He's almost always listening to music. He's come to accept that his life has value and wants you to know yours does too. He writes poems and makes collages in Austin, TX, where he supervises adolescents with developmental impairments.

Pate Conway —

Mary Beth Frezon
    Quilter and painter,
    Herder of cats, love fruitcake,
    Writer of Haiku

Gay Guard-Chamberlin lives in Chicago but visits any place and time in this world and any others whenever she wants through art and poetry.

Carmen Kennedy I create small collages on paper and larger works on wood and canvas. My work is inspired by meditation, everyday life, and Art history. I create worlds for images to interact. Sometimes the worlds stand on their own. BFA Art History, BA Studio Art, The University of Texas at Austin.

Fascinated since childhood by the power of words and pictures to convey meaning and arouse emotion, **Carol A. Keslar** writes, photographs, and collages to tell stories of identity and life passages. A former marketing and communication executive, she currently lives in Oakland, California.

Like many of the August postcard poets, **Tanya Korigan** enjoys the visual aspect of the sent and received sheaves immensely. The sketching furthers the simple power of sharing where you are.

L. Lisa Lawrence is a multimedia artist and performer with a passion for pottery, painting, photography, dance and written word. She finds magic and inspiration in nature and connecting with those who read/view her art. When not creating, she is most often found in nature. Her website is wildcelticrose.net.

Doris Lynch has published poems, stories, and haibun in various literary magazines. Finishing Line Press published her chapbook *Praising Invisible Things*. Her young adult biography on Tolkien was published by Scholastic Press. This is her first published photograph. She works as a community librarian and reviews books for *Library Journal*.

Tim Mateer I practice curiosity in Austin, Texas. Performing, writing, and directing in the theater, dance, and film industries for 40 years. I am a 3-year participant in Poetry Postcard Month. Sharing in this creative partnership, and the challenge of writing in the moment daily is an inspiration. Thank you all.

Amy Miller recently returned to art after having the enthusiasm beaten out of her by art school in the 1980s. She takes photos of natural objects and fishing debris. She is developing several of her kayaking photos into a series of linocut prints featuring southern Oregon lakes and mountains.

Paul E. Nelson See Editor biography

Kelleyanne Pearce is a postcard poet in the Pacific Northwest, which gives her inspiration and peace and is the place her soul is meant to be. She enjoys collaging, writing, and hiking. She considers her collage art to be a place for found objects left behind to find new relevance.

Dairine Pearson lives a wonder-filled life in Santa Barbara, California.

Eugenia Hepworth Petty is a writer, photographer, and mixed media artist based in the Pacific Northwest. Galleries and a list of publication credits may be found at: www.eugeniahepworth.com.

Laura L. Snyder has been exuberant about the August Postcard swap for the last five years! Primarily known as a poet, this is Laura's first jaunt into the world of collage. Find her latest poems in *Claudius Speaks, Poetry Breakfast*, and in *Windfall*. Laura creates between clouds in Seattle.

Abhaya Thomas lives in unincorporated NW Portland Oregon on a small farm. Here, along with her husband, she raised four children, an occasional dairy goat and hopefully her consciousness. There have been a few artistic endeavors thrown in the mix. This is her first published work.

Joanna Thomas is a visual artist and poet residing in Ellensburg, WA. She is a founding member of PUNCH, an artist-run gallery previously located (2006-2016) in the Pioneer Square district of Seattle. Her poems have appeared in *Otoliths, Picture Sentence, Found Poetry Review, and shufPoetry*. In 2016 she founded the Inland Poetry Prowl (www.inlandpoetry.com).

Matt Trease is an artist and IT Analyst living in Seattle, WA. His poems have appeared recently in *Nautilus Review, Apricity, Hotel Amerika,* and *Phoebe*. He is the author of the chapbook *Later Heaven: Production Cycles*, and he co-runs the Margin Shift reading series in Seattle's Belltown neighborhood.

Editors

A Pushcart nominee and winner of the 2016 Ken Warfel Fellowship, **J.I. Kleinberg, Editor,** is co-editor of *Noisy Water: Poetry from Whatcom County, Washington* (Other Mind Press 2015). Her poetry has appeared recently in *One, Diagram, Otoliths, Raven Chronicles,* and elsewhere. She lives in Bellingham, Washington, and blogs most days at chocolateisaverb.wordpress.com and thepoetrydepartment.wordpress.com.

Poet/interviewer **Project Founder and Editor Paul E. Nelson** founded SPLAB & the Cascadia Poetry Festival, published: *American Sentences* (Apprentice House 2015); *A Time Before Slaughter* (Apprentice House, shortlisted for a 2010 Genius Award by *The Stranger*) and *Organic in Cascadia: A Sequence of Energies* (essay, Lumme Editions, Brazil, 2013). He's interviewed Allen Ginsberg, Michael McClure, Sam Hamill, José Kozer, Robin Blaser, Nate Mackey, Joanne Kyger, George Bowering, Brenda Hillman and Daphne Marlatt, presented poetry/poetics in London, Brussels, Qinghai & Beijing, China, and published work in *Golden Handcuffs Review, Zen Monster* and *Hambone*. Awarded *The Capilano Review's* 2014 Robin Blaser Award, he writes an American Sentence every day.

Managing Editor Ina Roy-Faderman's poems appear in *Right Hand Pointing*, the Tupelo 30/30 Project, and *WhatRoughBeast*, among others; recent recognitions include *Richmond Anthology of Poetry* Best Poem award and a Pushcart nomination for fiction. Educated at Stanford (MD) and UCBerkeley (PhD), she teaches bioethics at university, helps edit *Rivet Journal*, and runs the library at a school for gifted kids. Her personal life revolves around small-mammal wrangling, postcard poems, and coffee. More at www.inafelltoearth.com.

David Seaver (Cover Design) has a degree in engineering, which may explain a lot. Most of the time, he does visual and UI design in Silicon Valley. In his off hours, he lifts weights, exasperates the cats, and makes things.

www.ingramcontent.com/pod-product-compliance
Lightning Source LLC
Chambersburg PA
CBHW041503010526
44118CB00001B/7